C.A.R.E.

Communicate
Assist
Respect
Empower

A Holistic Approach to Caregiving

JoAnn Freeborn

Family Care and Concern, LLC

C.A.R.E.

Communicate – Assist – Respect – Empower

A Holistic Approach to Caregiving

Family Care and Concern, LLC – Publisher

Library of Congress Control Number: 2013954158

ISBN – 978-0-9910591-1-9
1. Caregiving 2. Eldercare 3. Aging

Cover Artwork: Kimberly Baker
Cover Design: AZ Publishing Services, LLC

Printed in the United States of America

www.familycareandconcern.com

DEDICATION

C.A.R.E. is dedicated to my dear mother, Urcel Jury Young, who loved me unconditionally and inspired me to live a life of care and concern for others.

This book is also dedicated to all caregivers who place quality of life and meaningful relationships above all else.

ACKNOWLEDGMENTS

During the writing of this book and for the fifty-four years we have been married, I have been fortunate to have enjoyed the endless support and encouragement of my husband, Richard.

I am deeply grateful to my precious children; Julie, Kim and Rick, and their partners who enthusiastically cheered me on toward my goal. They and my seven grandchildren are the most valuable legacy I will leave on Earth.

A special thanks to PJ Hultstrand and Papu Maniar for their technical and design assistance.

Much gratitude to Beverly Scroggins for her editing expertise and an abundance of valuable life lessons learned.

I give a respectful nod to Robert G. Dicus, PT, and Co-Founder of the Therapeutic Associates Physical Therapy, who inspired me to know my potential. And, to Richard Massa, former head of the Department of Communications at Missouri Southern State College, who taught me the value of doing all that I believe in with PASSION.

Finally, I am grateful to the Neosho Jaycee Wives of Neosho, Missouri for my selection as a former Neosho Outstanding Woman of the Year and to Missouri Southern State University for being honored with the Annie Baxter Women in Government Award.

TABLE OF CONTENTS

Chapter 1

OLD HOME MOVIES

I shifted from side to side and felt the cool sheet on my shoulder. It took me a moment to figure out where I was. Then, the sound of the surf crashing on the shore and the scent of a salty sea breeze wafting in through the bedroom window reminded me that we were all gathered at the beach to celebrate the wonderful life of my mother, Urcel.

As I listened to children's laughter, I breathed in the aroma of coffee brewing in the kitchen, and lay back on my pillow reflecting upon the events that had brought us to this place.

I remembered the day a few weeks before mom died when she suggested the "beach party." It hadn't come as a surprise. Mom had always loved parties. She was usually the instigator, the planner, the hostess and one of the most exuberant participants. She often remarked, "Let's come up with a reason to have a party." The planning would then begin.

For mom, a party could be a group of neighbors enjoying a drink on the patio after a busy day working in their yards. It could be the annual family Independence Day celebration around our pool. It was more of an attitude than anything. Attitude was always an important ingredient in the way mom approached everything in life. We still get calls from Aunt Jean on the Fourth of July saying, "The Fourth never passes that I don't think of Urcel's great pool parties!"

During her last days, mom and I had some interesting

conversations about dreams. Mom insisted that she didn't dream. I told her I had read that we all dream. It is just a question of whether we remember them or not. I shared with her that when I became interested in dreams, I actively began remembering my own by trying to recall them immediately when waking and it had worked. A few weeks later she told me she had been trying to do the same thing but the only ones she remembered were times when she was at a party! I was not surprised.

In keeping with her request, family and friends from all over the country were gathered together at the beach to celebrate mom's life.

The aroma of coffee and the fresh sea breeze pulled me back from my morning reverie. As I returned to the moment, I said a silent prayer of thanksgiving, climbed out of bed, walked to the bathroom and splashed water on my face. I looked in the mirror and couldn't help notice my mother's sweet face looking back at me. I smiled and she smiled back. She was with me still. With a quick wink, I headed out to the kitchen to have a cup of coffee with those who had come to continue sharing our life experience.

Mom had been wise in encouraging us to wait awhile to plan a beach party to celebrate her life. We had not been in the mood to party in those first days and weeks following her death. My body and spirit were weary and my heart empty without her physical presence. It was truly a time to grieve our loss and to begin renewing our strength. Come summer, we would all "gather together at the beach" as she had asked us to do.

A long journey of love, sharing and support had finally come to an end. My mother passed away at 88 years of age; her life was good and complete. Although her final years were tainted with the dreaded Alzheimer's disease, she remained a pillar of strength and an inspiration to us all. She lived with dignity

4

right up to the very end, experiencing her family's loving comfort even in the final days of her life when she received a "spa treatment" as we called it. Just hours before she left us, she lay in her Hospice bed receiving a gentle body rub with her favorite scented body lotion.

In the days following her death, I sought to fill the void and take comfort in reminiscing as I watched old home movies of our family's journey through the years. As the familiar images passed before my eyes, I saw a lifelong connection, one that evolved through the years toward the ultimate caring close relationship I shared with my precious mom.

For as long as I can remember, my friends and family have all called me a born caregiver. I'm not quite sure what that means, but I have always taken it as a compliment. As I viewed the old images of our family's caring journey, I came to a new realization about how a person really becomes an effective caregiver. In fact, what I believe the films truly revealed was not a "born caregiver" but a child who had been nurtured in a culture of care, rich in the very qualities that are essential to effective caregiving: **C**ommunication, **A**ssistance, **R**espect and **E**mpowerment.

Each of us enters this world with the natural need to be cared for and to care. In most families we are nurtured in the qualities essential to effective caregiving. However, by the time we are called upon to care for our aging parents or others, a gradual disconnect has often occurred in family relationships. This disconnect can make it difficult to reach out, to communicate and to make effective healthcare decisions and lifestyle choices.

While I watched familiar images in the movie frames pass before my eyes, I began to see how I grew in an environment of love and trust and stayed connected to my family. Although the film was

black and white and grainy, I could see myself as a four-year old cradling a doll that my daddy, just home from World War II, had placed in my arms. A few frames later I was kissing my elderly Grandfather on the cheek. Then on the next reel, there I was at eight, proudly holding my newborn baby brother, Jackie, in my arms for the neighborhood kids to admire. That was back in the 40s when we didn't take newborn babies out in public. So, my Mother set me up by the dining room window with Jackie on my lap so that my friends could come by and see him. As he grew, it was apparent that a deep bond was developing as I rocked him in his cradle, pushed him in his backyard swing and held his hand while walking him to school.

As our family story continued to reveal itself on film, I witnessed myself brushing my paternal Grandmother

Helen's long, thinning hair as she sat in her dressing gown before the mirror of her vanity table. I remembered the sweetness of her face. She stayed with me when I was a preschooler during the time my mommy had to go to work at Benson's dress shop while my daddy was away in the Army. I recalled how she made gorgeous braided rugs out of her old nylon stockings. There is a picture of our whole family at the dinner table eating her wonderful pot roast. I only wish there was a picture of the time the pressure cooker blew up with the pot roast in it. What a mess. The kitchen was a sight to see, but the pot roast remained deliciously mouthwatering!

My grandmother was a very large lady. I suspect my lifelong struggle with weight could have a genetic predisposition from her DNA. I wish now I had possessed the wisdom at thirteen to ask her the many questions about her early life I have wondered about through subsequent years. Unfortunately, she died suddenly of a cerebral hemorrhage, and I was robbed of the chance to know her from an adult perspective and to hear about her life as a young girl. Perhaps the lost opportunity to know her more fully was a contributing factor to my growing belief that I should take every opportunity to connect with those I love and fully share our life experiences.

I continued to sift and sort through the reels of old film. I married my husband Richard, a wonderful man and my own family began to take shape. We had two little girls and then a little boy. Caregiving for me would now take on an entirely new meaning. Caring for your own children has its own unique dynamic. I became acutely aware the intense daily caregiving tasks of raising children are all directed toward a relatively specific goal – the development of a mature adult capable of fully independent function – while the goal of caregiving in later years is to provide support, comfort and encouragement during time of change and challenge.

Nonetheless, raising my own family shaped and strengthened skills I would use again and again throughout my life.

Early one morning when I fired up the projector, I was delighted to see Pappy, my grandfather, in his wheelchair. My two year old daughter, Julie, was riding on his lap. After Pappy, my dad's father, suffered a stroke and was paralyzed, he came to live with us. For three years, my mother provided direct, hands on care by bathing, feeding and turning him in bed to prevent bedsores. She even brought his nightly "nip" of favorite whiskey!

One of my early observations was that our family relationships continued uninterrupted and Pappy's needs were easily incorporated into the family routine. While my mother was the primary caregiver, my dad played a critical, supportive role, and extended family members were occasionally called in to provide respite. Pappy's presence in our home, with his great sense of humor and tales from the past, added to the richness of the fabric of our family. Emotions were vented, feelings shared,

When Pappy died, we grieved. There was a great sense of emptiness. We missed him, but our whole family had grown from having shared Pappy's life experience. I believe we were all better people for having cared for Pappy.

The next scenes on the old films were images of the day my mom's Mother came to live with my parents. We affectionately called her Granny Clara. Richard and I lived nearby and participated in her care and have daily interaction with her. Granny was quite a storyteller and that is how I came to learn much more about my family history and its legacy of family caring that contributed to the woman I am

today.

During the years Granny Clara lived with my folks, we experienced her grace, her wit, her tenacity and her patience. I suspect that my love of writing poetry might have come from her. Clearly, my natural tendencies toward caregiving were being further strengthened as I observed <u>my</u> mother caring for <u>her</u> mother.

Granny Clara came from French Canadian ancestry. In the late 1800s her father farmed in northern Wisconsin and made a living shearing sheep. She was called "Tommy" because she was the "Tom Boy" in her family! After completing normal school (a school created to train high school graduates to be teachers), Clara went to a dance at a friend's farm. There she met Frank whom she later married. Soon after their marriage, Frank broke his ankle while working at his job on the railroad. During the long winter while he was recovering, Clara taught school at the Lac Vieux Desert Indian Reservation where she was called

"Kenamagaque." Many years later when my mom and I visited the site of the old log school house where Granny had taught, I told the old Chief that Granny Clara said the name meant "teacher." He smiled and said, "In the Chippewa language it meant "Woman Who Knows."

Clara later devoted herself to raising seven daughters among whom my mother was the eldest. Following the Great Depression, she was instrumental in holding her family together and building a new future. As she demonstrated repeatedly throughout her life, she was truly "a woman who knew."

Granny Clara - strong, feisty and fun-loving - would spend the final seventeen years of her life living with my folks. During the first several years she participated actively in the household routine. Toward the end of her 96 years, she remained an honored presence at every gathering although she no longer washed dishes or helped with the cooking! The enduring gift we all received from her was the connection to our family roots.

Throughout the years that my mother cared for Granny, I again observed something very central to my mother's style. Granny's needs were always addressed as an integral part of our whole family. My mother never sacrificed disproportionately or martyred herself to meet Granny's needs. She had an inner sense of the importance of taking care of herself in order to be able to meet the needs of anyone else. Obviously, my mother's healthy approach to her role as caregiver is one reason why she was able to carry it out so successfully over so many years. Observing her well balanced approach contributed to shaping my holistic view of family care.

As I continued my journey through the old home movies, the images passing before my eyes became difficult to view for they were scenes of the days following my little brother Jack's horrible, untimely death. He had just returned safely from Vietnam, only to have his young life of 26 years cruelly snuffed out in a fatal motorcycle accident. Caregiving took an urgent new turn for me.

The call telling us that Jack had been killed came during the dinner hour. With Richard's help, plane reservations were made. By midnight, after my long journey across the country, I was with my parents, trying to comfort them. The two broken-hearted bodies I saw clinging to each other as I descended the walkway from the airplane crushed my heart. As I hugged them to me and shared their grief, I knew my mission was to encourage them to face the challenge of living again. This was the most important way I could care for them at the time.

The next series of films recalled for me a tumultuous life changing time of great stress and personal growth. Interestingly, not a lot of pictures were taken. It was not a time when picture taking held a high priority. However, the few pictures I see continue to show a tightly knit family holding on to one another as we struggled with serious illness. The old home movies clearly showed that I had lived through many difficult experiences in my relatively young life but they would now reveal a time that would challenge me beyond my imagination. When I was thirty-three, during a single year, my husband's parents John and Thelma were both diagnosed with terminal cancer, Mother with breast cancer and dad with prostate cancer.

The few films from this period of our lives clearly reveal how my early childhood nurturing shaped my response to these challenges. The growing need to share our common human experience is certainly reflected in the way we reacted during those health care crises. Terrible as it was to receive the news of their terminal cancer, our immediate concern was characteristic of our natures. Our only desire at this time of crisis was to reach out to Mom and Dad, to express our desire to share in this

experience and to provide whatever support they might need.

Our daughters, Julie and Kim, were teenagers and our son, Rick, was in elementary school. My husband Richard had just been laid off from his job in aerospace, and I was working part time at our local church. With some of the most challenging times occurring within the life of our own family, we were now faced with caring for Richard's terminally ill parents during their last years. Needless to say, at the outset we were emotionally blown away by the immensity of it all

As we contemplated these daunting challenges, every fiber of my being resounded with a deep call to care for our aging parents in the same loving way they had cared for us as children. It was my desire for our whole family to share their experience and to comfort and encourage them to live life fully and meaningfully.

The caregiving journey took us careening down rocky slopes and up steep paths we never would have thought we could climb. This journey also took us down dead end roads and sent us on time consuming detours. Conflicts in scheduling between our children's and our parent's needs found us meeting one another coming and going. Then, just when we felt we would all drown in the raging tempest of frustration, we would be gifted with the renewed energy that comes with the dawn of each new day.

On the movie screen in front of me, a scene that caught my attention was one of our two teenage daughters sitting with their grandparents in our family room watching American Bandstand together on TV. The next images show Julie and Kim carefully arranging their Grandmother Thelma's wig as she prepares to model in a church fashion show. Wow, what a picture! She had lost all her hair during chemotherapy, but still wanted to be in the church fashion show. These are the times that make it all worthwhile!

The films that followed, taken at their funerals, reminded me again of just how young I was, thirty two, and how unprepared I was to be helping my husband prepare for his parents funerals. With John and Thelma's passing we reached the final destination of this particular caregiving journey. There was no question that it had been worthwhile. Though it had not been without some struggle and some conflict, the rewards far outweighed the cost.

While sharing my story, I believe that it is vital to point out there are no right or wrong ways to accomplish meaningful caregiving. In various circumstances with a range of options, our family often saw things from differing perspectives. The central element of how we made our decisions, however, was that everyone was motivated toward our loved one's well-being. Then, we communicated our feelings, considered our options, made choices and moved forward. Everyone was not always completely satisfied with the outcome, but early on we had decided to face these things as a family unit. So, nobody "picked up their marbles and went home mad." We all respected each other and moved forward the best we could. A less than perfect solution to a problem is not a failure; it is life. We chose to go through it together.

During the journey of caring for Richard's mom and dad, I learned some extremely valuable life lessons about the nature of caring and how caregivers are not just born but are shaped by our life experience and changing personal perspective. I also grew grown in my understanding of the importance of nurturing our interpersonal relationships as a central part of effective caregiving.

As we grieved and began to heal from our loss of Richard's folks, I began to look back on the past six years with them and assess the whole experience. Though, overall, we felt tremendously enriched by the caring journey we had shared, we often encountered roadblocks along the way. In retrospect, I increasingly came to believe that difficult communications were at the heart most of our struggles. We <u>struggled</u> as we tried to communicate with each other and Mom and Dad about making mutually beneficial care decisions. We <u>struggled</u> as we tried to communicate with doctors, nurses and social workers. We <u>struggled</u> as we tried to communicate with a limited and fragmented service delivery system. Though we <u>struggled</u> in so many ways, at the core of our ability to endure and succeed was always our respectful commitment to a shared life of quality and dignity.

My reflections about what we faced while caring for Richard's parents began to make me think about how the lessons we had learned could help smooth the way for others who faced similar challenges. When our physical selves became re-energized and my proverbial "cup" began to refill, I made a personal commitment that I would devote my renewed energy to helping other families in their efforts to care for their loved ones.

The next movies provided an interesting, happy interlude and certainly made for wonderful memories. There I am in cap and gown, a college graduate at forty-seven! In the audience were my proud mother, husband, children and grandchildren. I reflected on how we arrived at this happy event, and I recalled the life altering decision that brought me here.

In an endeavor to achieve my goal, I returned to school and earned a Bachelor's Degree in Communications. Then, I pursued a career in Social Services with Missouri's Region Ten Area Agency on Aging. Over the next several years as a social worker I enjoyed the opportunity to help many families negotiate the turbulent waters of caregiving. Later as Executive Director of the Area Agency on Aging, I served as a statewide advocate on behalf of frail elders at risk and their families.

I was able to institute many improvements in a fragmented service delivery system. Most importantly, I developed a life changing, holistic model of family care. The development and implementation of this holistic model of family care was based on strengthening family relationships leading to proactive, collaborative family planning. Ultimately, this approach to caregiving is far more rewarding than simply the typical interventionist response to a health care crisis.

Sharing the message about this holistic model of family caregiving remains my life's passion today. There is no doubt that during the care giving journey for our parents we faced many, many challenges regarding obtaining quality services and healthcare for them. However, the biggest challenge we and most families face, is working together collaboratively to explore and make decisions about healthcare and lifestyle options that will result in mutually beneficial solutions.

In my years as a social worker, I never had to comfort families grieving over dirty dishes in the sink or unmopped floors. However, I have comforted many families grieving over broken relationships and things left unsaid. Thus, it is the quality of our interpersonal interactions that I believe should be at the heart of how we care for one another. When our caregiving journey is over, at the end of our time together, it will not be the quality of home care services that we will remember, but the times we shared together that will linger in our hearts.

The last few reels in the dwindling pile held significant meaning for me. In these final films I saw a time when my caregiving skills were challenged as they had never been before. It was while I viewed the images of this challenge that the seed was planted to share the story of our family's journey of care.

When I first started watching these old home movies, the pictures were in black and white. Then they changed to color. What a new dimension that added! However, even though the quality of the film improved and the pictures showed the passage of time, our moving from place to place and our lives progressing, it was apparent that in spite of changing circumstances the culture of caring through our continued family connection remained constant.

When I first started watching these old home movies, the pictures were in black and white. Then they changed to color. What a new dimension that added! However, even though the quality of the film improved and the pictures showed the passage of time, our moving from place to place and our lives progressing, it was apparent that in spite of changing circumstances the culture of caring through our continued family connection remained constant.

The last reels of my old home movies show me assuming an active role in caring for my own parents. My birth father had passed away suddenly of a heart attack at a young age, and a few years later, Mom married Fred, an old family friend. They chose to settle near Richard and

25

me. They enjoyed an active and happy "Third Age." During their twenty six wonderful years together, we built a mutually beneficial relationship. Toward the end of this time, the value of a family centered model of care was truly tested and validated. When the sure signs of Alzheimer's disease could no longer be ignored, we received a formal diagnosis, and my mother began her "long goodbye."

All my caregiving instincts once again kicked in along with my acquired knowledge, skills and experience. Yet, in the final analysis, it was only through a deliberate and determined family collaboration of hearts and minds that we provided the quality of care that my mom so richly deserved. The holistic model of family care that I had developed and used in my professional career was fully life tested on my own dear mother.

Chapter 2

C.A.R.E.

A HOLISTIC APPROACH TO CAREGIVING

I would like to share this innovative approach to caregiving in the hope that it will inspire you to move toward a richer, more meaningful, shared life experience with your family members, regardless of their ages. As I reflected on my life journey through old family movies, I realized, that I had not been observing a "born caregiver," but a future caregiver who grew up in a loving family and was nurtured in the essential qualities of effective and mutually beneficial caregiving. These valuable qualities would later translate into caring relationships throughout my life. It is not just the giving of physical care, but the respectful and tolerant sharing of our different perspectives that constitutes truly successful caring and results in genuine contentment.

If you reflect upon these thoughts, you may come to realize that you also grew up in such a family and you need only to refresh and strengthen your natural and learned skill to develop renewed approach to caregiving. On the other hand, you may be ready to reshape your views entirely.

Traditional models of care giving focus primarily on interventionist responses at a time of critical need. These responses are principally to identify and put in place services to meet immediate needs at the time of a healthcare crisis. As a result of this type of intervention, difficulties typically surface for a variety of reasons.

A crisis situation, such as suffering a stroke, is obviously a time of natural stress. Families may have traveled great distances for a limited amount of time to deal with a crisis situation. Adult children and their elderly parents may be at cross purposes about what they want to achieve. Typically, families fail to have preliminary discussions about choices regarding their future needs. These simply aren't things people generally feel comfortable talking about. At the time of the critical incident, the parent is desperately afraid of losing control of his or her independence, while at the same time, the family is focused on securing immediate safety and well-being for their loved one.

The result is an experience that can be painful for everyone, resulting in a temporary solution only and ending up with the difficult experience being repeated. With this reactionary response, the focus is on meeting the immediate needs for physical care and not on the collaborative relationship that needs to be developed that would lead to long term success.

Dictionaries frequently define care as a "feeling of interest in, or concern for someone." This definition is a much broader and more meaningful concept than the narrow view of just putting supportive or health services in place to meet physical care needs. My family's experience led me to begin encouraging others to consider an alternative, more holistic concept of caring. This approach involves an ongoing, proactive process rather than a reactionary response. The outcome is a more richly rewarding for the whole family.

The concept of family care I recommend focuses on the dynamics of family interactions and employs the four key components of **C**ommunication, **A**ssistance, **R**espect and **E**mpowerment – **C.A.R.E**. Through the implementation of these components of care, families will create an environment of trust and understanding within which all family members can comfortably explore and make decisions about healthcare and lifestyle options together.

From the beginning of time, the family of man has shared itself with one another as naturally as our breath. Family has always been at the center of life's experience. From the moment we enter this world we are surrounded by caring family, each milestone along our path is enriched by the sharing the experience. Happy times are more joyous; sorrow is lessened.

Rites of passage such as baptisms, graduations and weddings all provide opportunities to come together to touch each other and share the moment. While raising our children we establish the pattern of coming together when we face challenges or problems for counsel and encouragement. We talk it through and develop solutions. Certainly, our experience should be the same throughout our older adult years. This part of life's journey should not be traveled alone, isolated from the benefits of a shared human experience. For most of human history families have faced the challenges of aging together in this same loving and supportive way.

Toward the middle of the twentieth century, the way we age began to change. As we became a more mobile society after World War! Young adults crisscrossed the country seeking their fortune while their parents remained behind to "age in place." A new phenomenon also began to occur. The advent of modern medicine and improved healthcare fueled expectations of a longer life. With these expectations of longer life came expanded opportunities for older adults, including travel, relocation to retirement communities and even the establishment of new careers. The opportunity for older adults to live exciting and productive lives became increasingly important. We began to understand that this new "Third Age" may extend potentially twenty or thirty rich and rewarding years.

These new expectations meant that we might age in a very different way than our parents and grandparents. Historically, we aged in a downward linear pattern from productivity to frailty and death based on deteriorating health over a relatively short period of time. Noted demographer Ken Dykwald describes the way we are aging now as the "Agewave." Instead of aging in a steady downward pattern from health through frailty to death, we are likely to experience a series of lows related to health issues with recovery to improved health and renewed productivity. This creates a wave like pattern of aging that provides recurring opportunities for prolonged high quality of life in an extended "Third Age."

In light of the "Agewave" phenomenon, we should now view older adulthood as a series of dynamic phases that can range from high productivity to the need for care and assistance. As we move through the phases of continuity and change, those who age well will share their hopes and dreams with their families and plan for the future realistically together. This includes planning for contingencies during those times of change when healthcare issues may interrupt our current state of good health and well-being. And, if we live long enough we will inevitably experience losses of physical capabilities, social roles and jobs. Ultimately, the sharing of our experience with supportive family is the surest way to secure an older adulthood of dignity and respect with as much independence as possible. Key to the success of this process is making it a part of our shared life experience. Our quality of life will be greatly enriched for everyone.

Unfortunately, in their search to enjoy the opportunities available during this retirement, many older adults develop an unrealistic view that this newly found independence can last unchanged. They often struggle to protect it by disconnecting from the very families that have in earlier years been central to their lives. In their blind determination to resist change, a curious defense mechanism can kick in. There is almost an effort to "circle the wagons," "put our blinders on" and limit communication with the very loved ones with whom we have always shared our lives. We just want things to stay the same. We think if we just don't talk about it, nothing will change.

However, over the period of twenty or thirty years

leading to the end of life, the two things we can count on are change and, if we should live long enough that we will need some help. So let's explore **C**ommunication, **A**ssistance, **R**espect and **E**mpowerment, the four components of this holistic model of care that will help families move successfully through these periods of continuity and change that will inevitably be a part of older adulthood.

Chapter 3

COMMUNICATION
C. A. R. E. Component One

Communication, the first component in my holistic model of family care, may be the most critical, mediating variable in how successful any care giving effort will be. Studies show that families are able to adjust to change and difficult situations in direct proportion to their ability to communicate effectively with one another.

The ability to communicate effectively begins with a desire to be more sensitive to and understanding of each other's point of view. Effective communication requires a basic understanding of the communication process and the use of both appropriate speaking and listening skills. The use of effective communication techniques can improve the implementation of the other three components of family care: **A**ssistance, **R**espect, and **E**mpowerment.

Communication is most broadly defined as the generation and attribution of meaning between people. Ideally it happens in a circular process where one person (the sender) speaks to another person (the receiver) sending a message he hopes the receiver understands as he, the sender, meant it. If the receiver understands the message as the sender intended, then a shared meaning has been achieved and understanding has been created between two people. When a shared meaning or understanding is achieved between two people, we call this effective Communication.

However, creating a shared understanding or meaning can get tricky. We have all been in situations where we said something to someone, and they misunderstood what we meant to say. When this occurs, especially in a highly charged, emotional exchange between family members, feelings get hurt and the communication ceases. There are lots of reasons why the communication process between people can break down, but first let's look at how we avoid misunderstandings in the ideal circular communication process.

In the ideal circular communication process, the receiver and the sender enter into a series of respectful questions and answers to provide what is referred to as feedback. Feedback provides clarification and results in the desired shared meaning. The outcome is shared understanding or effective communication.

When we think about our communication with another person, it is important to keep a few basic things in mind. First, it is impossible to not communicate! The very effort to not communicate communicates something. Through body language, tone of voice, gestures and even facial expressions we constantly communicate with others, whether we think we are or not.

Secondly, the effect of a communication is irreversible. Once something has been said or expressed it cannot be taken back. We can attempt to correct a miscommunication, but it cannot be erased.

Thirdly, because of the number of variables involved, communication is complex. It is said that there are six people involved in any communication: 1) who you think you are; 2) who you think the other person is; 3) who you think the other person thinks you are; 4) who the other person thinks he/she is; 5) who the other person thinks you are and 6) who the other person thinks you think he/she is.

Finally, communication is contextual. This means that it doesn't happen in isolation. The psychological context of the communication includes the personality, values and emotional state of both participants. The relational context refers to the way we react to the other person. Examples include parent/child, employee/subordinate or trusting/suspicious. The situational context deals with the psycho-social environment "where" the conversation occurs. Conversations that take place in formal offices are likely to be very different than those that occur in familiar, relaxed settings. The environmental context describes things such as the furniture in the room, the temperature and the time of day. Cultural elements such as uncomfortability with close proximity and direct eye contact can all affect our interactions.

With an awareness of the multitude of things that can impact the outcome of a communication, it's no wonder so many communications fail. In the context of trying to care for a family member, it is almost always ineffective communication that is the shaky foundation of most troubled care giving relationships. Therefore, let's consider how to improve our family communication so that when we deal healthcare or lifestyle issues, our ability to communicate effectively will enable us to explore options together resulting in mutually beneficial choices.

The "Golden Rule" is really a good place to start. "Do unto others as you would have others do unto you." Or, going back to the basics of effective communications, we each need to "have a desire to be more sensitive to each other's point of view." One basic human need is simply to be better understood and this is where becoming a better listener takes on increased importance.

A few guiding principles will insure a more positive outcome to your family communications: 1) select a time and setting that encourages a relaxed and comfortable interaction, 2) try to establish an environment of trust and empathy, 3) eliminate distractions such noise, pain, hunger and interruptions, 4) position yourself in comfortable proximity, face to face on the same level, 5) speak in a moderate tone of voice, enunciating clearly, for even when there is a hearing impairment it is usually not loudness that helps and 6) hold preliminary discussions allowing time to think before making final decisions.

COMMUNICATION TECHNIQUES

VERBAL APPROACHES:

- Use calm normal voice pattern.
- Speak to a loved one as a peer, not a child.
- Phrase open-ended questions, one at a time.
- Wait for a response.
- Don't interrupt.
- Use specific, positive phrases. (We'll work through this together!)
- Validate feelings with verbal response. (I see, I understand)

NONVERBAL APPROACHES:

- Establish and maintain eye contact.
- Remember your facial expressions reflect your attitude and mood.
- Lean slightly forward in an open body position,

arms unfolded.

- Nod head to indicate agreement.
- Use touch when comfortable and appropriate.
- Make body movements slowly.
- Smile.

HELPFUL WORDS AND PHRASES

- Thank You.
- You're Welcome.
- I Love You.

VALIDATING PHRASES:

- Please.
- I understand how you must feel.
- I might feel that way too in your situation.
- I can see this is very important to you.
- This is what I hear you saying.
- Tell me more about it.
- Share your ideas with me.

COOPERATING AND COMPROMISING PHRASES:

- I gather you don't agree. Share with me the reason for your objection.
- Let's see how we can reach our mutual goal.
- You see it differently. Let's see if we can work through our differences.
- Let's try to find a solution that works well for both of us.
- Let's put the subject to rest awhile and talk about it again later.

COMMUNICATION BARRIERS:

- Language
- Cultural background
- Personal experience
- Educational level
- Environmental factors (noise, temperature, location)
- Relational issues (trust vs. mistrust)
- Personal bias

- Emotional state (anger, depression)

- Feelings (pain, fear, frustration)

- Health issues (illness, medication effects)

COMMUNICATION WITH SENSORY IMPAIRED INDIVIDUALS

HEARING IMPAIRED

- Speak clearly and slowly (don't yell).

- Carefully articulate consonants.

- Keep volume of voice even and moderate.

- Use a lower tone of voice.

- Position yourself within three feet and in good light.

- Use gestures and hand signals.

- If not understood, don't just repeat; say it in a different way.

VISION IMPAIRED

- Identify your presence when you enter.

- Never rearrange familiar objects.

- Speak naturally.

- Speak before you touch a person.

- Avoid nonverbal cues.

- Don't count on facial expressions to convey a message.

- If you hand a person something, speak before you place it in their hands.

- Announce your departure.

SPEECH IMPAIRED

- Don't assume a person doesn't understand because they can't speak.

- Suggest and provide materials for written response.

- Develop a method of using signals.

MEMORY IMPAIRED

- Accept that each encounter may be a new experience.

- Avoid quizzing or testing memory.

- Don't argue over forgotten details.

47

- Write things down.

- Use labels and written directions. (Keep it simple)

- Use pictures and written life stories.

- Explore the use of Validation or Reality Therapy. Reality Therapy focuses on keeping the person based in real time. Validation Therapy accepts the person's unrealistic perceptions. Both have value depending on a person's level of dementia.

LISTENING

Listening is at the heart of effective communication and therefore at the heart of all human relationships. Listening helps develop an understanding of how the other person feels. In the context of family communication, understanding how the other person feels can give us the insight that may help us move toward mutually beneficial interaction.

Nature gave us two ears and only one tongue, which

should be a gentle hint that listening is more important than talking. It has been said that no one has ever learned anything while they were talking. A good way to begin listening is to substitute our own ego for a sense of humility. This is very much in keeping with the goal of effective communication, *"try to be more sensitive to each other's point of view"* and to the fundamental definition of a caring, *"to have a sense of concern for one another."* It has been said that listening to another's soul is a condition of disclosure and discovery and may be almost the greatest service that any human being may ever perform for another.

As an element of the circular communication process, listening provides the opportunity to give and receive critically important feedback. As stated earlier, through feedback we receive clarification and move toward our goal of shared understanding or effective communications.

LISTENING TECHNIQUES

DO

- Be quiet.

- Show openness and positive interest.

- Seek clarification.

- Listen for feelings which are neither right nor wrong, they just are.

- Think before responding.

- Listen for meaning not just words (There are 14,000 meanings for 500 most common words, an average of 28 meanings per word!)

DON'T

- Pass judgment in advance.

- Interrupt.

- Argue.

- Jump to conclusions.

- Assume.

- Be afraid of silence.

- Overreach.

FAMILY CONFERENCES

Most family communication occurs one on one and these conversations are often the least threatening and the most productive. However, there are times when it becomes necessary for families to hold a family conference. A family conference can be very effective if it is well planned and carefully executed. All of the above techniques should of course be taken into consideration. Additionally, the conference should be well planned and certain ground rules should be established.

GROUND RULES

- A facilitator should be selected.
- Everyone should speak for himself/herself.
- Establish goals for the family conference.
- There will be no interruptions.
- Discussion will be non-judgmental, without blame or criticism.
- Take turns speaking.

- Use "I" or "I feel", not "you" messages:

  Don't say, "You insist on walking without your cane."

  Say, "I feel frightened when you walk without your cane"

- Discussion should include:

  - Brainstorming.

  - Validation of feelings.

  - Establishment of trust and hope.

  - Exploration of options.

- Summarize areas of agreement and issues yet to be resolved.

- Express appreciation to each other for willingness to participate.

When I reflect on my own family caregiving experience in the old home movies, I saw us in communication with one another in good times and bad. Over time, as we moved back and forth across the country and from one stage of life to another, we stayed in touch and maintained communication no matter how difficult or uncomfortable the process became. Continuity of effort is a positive characteristic of effective communication that doesn't get a lot of attention. However, it may be central to why families who communicate effectively through the various phases of life move more easily through difficult times.

The older adults I have seen who aged most successfully and truly enjoyed their continued independence are individuals who regularly communicated with their families about their changing life circumstances. Even though everyone was not always in agreement, that was not a requirement of a good relationship. The challenge for older adults and their families is to use the four components of **C.A.R.E.:** **C**ommunication, **A**ssistance, **R**espect and **E**mpowerment to explore and develop options and choices to meet our changing needs over time and accept varying levels of success.

COMMUNICATING WITH TERMINALLY ILL FAMILY MEMBERS

Communicating with terminally ill family members presents especially sensitive challenges and rewards. Just as we know that effective communication enhances overall family relationships, our rational selves would have to believe that no one should have to face terminal illness and death in isolation. Yet, the reality of the matter is that a communication breakdown frequently occurs during this critical life phase.

Studies indicate that sensitive and effective communications can help a person facing a terminal illness who is dealing with a unique set of problems and circumstances. Our conflicting fears and emotions regarding death can lead to paralyzing communication apprehension. Until very recently, Western norms have dictated that we avoid the topic of death in polite conversation. The difficult circumstances faced by a family member with a terminal illness are all compounded by the tendency to avoid its discussion at all costs.

Early evidence of a communication breakdown may be exhibited when physicians fail to live up to their moral obligation by not communicating to the patient and family the terminal nature of the patient's condition. According to recent polls, 85% of people want to be told about the nature of their illness.

The tendency to avoid discussion at all cost continues on the part of family members. Taking their cue from the doctor, a pattern of denial begins. Possibly as a result of their own feelings of inadequacy and apprehension, the family contributes to the expansion of the widening communication gap and their loved one's isolation.

The fears of the terminally ill person fall into three basic categories: 1) the fear of pain and suffering, 2) the fear of leaving one's loved ones behind and 3) the fear of entering into an unknown realm.

Communicating these fears is an important part of coming to grips with them. People who are dying feel less isolated if they can share their feelings. Some patients suffer more from emotional isolation than from approaching death itself.

Cicely Saunders, one of the early founders of the Hospice movement, says "Despite myriad fears, death is not frightening when it is near to the patient who has been allowed to approach it in his own way."

Most terminally ill patients move through five stages: 1) denial, 2) anger, 3) bargaining, 4) depression, and 5) acceptance as they approach death. Open communication can facilitate the successful movement through these stages. During the terminal phase of an illness the patient typically experiences a growing need to share feelings with their closest family members.

The communication itself can be the stumbling block. Family members often back away because they don't know what to say or how to say it. The problem may well be with the word "say". Typically we focus too much on our need to say something. Remember, communication occurs in many ways. It is the often neglected communication technique of listening that is of key importance in communicating effectively with a terminally ill person.

Listening accomplishes two very important tasks. It provides the reassurance of one who cares and will not desert them and provides the caregiver with necessary clues as to what concerns the patient and how best to meet their needs. Studies have shown that an added benefit is that patients who are able to share their feelings openly and honestly with those they trust feel less physical pain.

Communication in its broadest context should be considered when dealing with a terminally ill loved one. The sound of family members communicating normally around them can be reassuring, as can the feel of loving hands arranging blankets.

As we approach death, we all bring with us certain unfinished business that needs to be resolved. Effective communication during this life phase provides opportunities to resolve differences and validate the worth of our lives. It is through the communication process that we have the opportunity to work through these final life challenges.

When those who are dying share information, they experience increased feelings of control, a greater sense of hope and an improved psychological response to treatment. The benefit to those sharing the experience is equally valuable and important. Grieving the loss of a loved one after death is both normal and necessary. However, the grieving process is often exaggerated and prolonged due to unexpressed and unresolved emotions. Family members who have shared fully in the experience of their terminally loved one generally come to terms with their death and pass through a normal grieving process of healing and adjustment.

An individual's right to die is as sacred as his right to live. How and where that death occurs is of great concern in our family centered model of **C.A.R.E.** When it is no longer possible to regain ones good health, improving the quality of our loved ones life remains an achievable goal.

It is important to remember that information is power and should not be feared or avoided. This model of **C.A.R.E.**, with its four components: **C**ommunication, **A**ssistance, **R**espect, and **E**mpowerment is not something done to someone but rather a process of shared planning and problem solving that family members enter into together repeatedly. Ideally, communication among all family members is occurring regularly. If regular communication is not occurring in your family, it is never too late to begin to improve family communications and in so doing, move toward a closer connection between family members.

Chapter 4

ASSISTANCE

C. A. R .E. Component Two

The second component of my holistic model of family care is Assistance. Obtaining appropriate health care and social services when needed is clearly a major consideration. Improved family communication will ultimately improve the process of choosing and accessing services needed by family members as they face choices regarding both opportunities and challenges. The goal in the context of a more holistic model of family care is to form patterns of family interaction that consider the potential for changing needs over time. Thus, if a critical healthcare event occurs, a tentative care plan is in place.

Currently, most families still enter into caregiving responsibilities at a time of critical need for assistance. The focus of immediate necessity is to find appropriate, supportive healthcare and social services and get them in place quickly. Unfortunately, in my first experience with family caregiving, I, too, was thrown into the role at a time of a major health care crisis.

Reflecting once again on the old home movies, I see us packing the car to make a 1,700 mile trip from Missouri to California to be with Richard's father at a time of crisis. He had been in the hospital for 45 days recovering from multiple surgeries and radiation related to the treatment of prostate cancer.

While in the doctor's office discussing Dad's care needs, the doctor informed us that Richard's mother's prognosis for further recovery from breast cancer the previous year was even more dire. Although the doctor suggested the probability of recovery for dad, he said mother would probably not survive another two years.

After much discussion and soul searching, we decided to invite them to come back to Missouri to live with us and face the challenges of their terminal illness together. They were grateful, and we all looked to the future optimistically. But the nature of the crisis situation had created added stress. Even in the most collaborative of families, there will always be moments fraught with stress and tension. Sometimes we just have to lower our expectations and not be so hard on ourselves or each other.

We loaded furniture and belongings into a big U-Haul truck and the folks into the car, and we headed home to two teenage daughters, an eight year old son and six years of caregiving that changed our lives.

It is critical to recognize that our choice to live with an extended family under one roof may not be the best choice for every family. The holistic model of family care that I encourage does not suggest specific lifestyle or healthcare choices. It is about family relationships and how families can work together to better make mutually beneficial decisions regarding these and other issues, to accept varying outcomes and to move on together. It is my hope that sharing our family experience may help other families move through the caregiving process with improved interpersonal skills and increased confidence so that the journey can be richly rewarding instead of just one to be endured.

Once we all got settled into our new living arrangements, we began to look for medical and social services we needed to help with Mom and Dad's care. We were certainly in for a rude awakening. Thirty years ago there simply was not the vast array of products and services that are available to caregivers today. The critical challenge we faced was finding services from a very limited set of options. Today that challenge is negotiating a vast service delivery system with varying eligibility and payment schemes.

When you are seeking help with care issues at a time of critical need, it is extremely valuable to have a single source of information and referral to the various service providers. The most effective source of reliable information is likely to be the local Area Agency on Aging (AAA) that serves your community. Developed under the authority of the Older Americans Act passed in 1965, over 600 AAAs have been established to coordinate services needed by older adults and their families. AAAs are listed in your phonebook under Community Services or Social Service Organizations. You can also call the Eldercare Locator's toll free number 1-800-677-1116 to find the nearest AAA. The AAA can refer you to a wide array of service providers as well as provide you with basic counseling services regarding the specific situation your family is facing. Hospital Social Workers may also be an excellent source of information regarding services that could be needed immediately following a hospitalization.

Throughout an expanded Third Age experience that may extend twenty to thirty years, there will be multiple issues to be explored and choices to be made. Since the focus of this book is the process of exploring options and making decisions, I will limit my effort to listing just a sampling of topics about which families are likely to need information.

COMMUNITY BASED RESOURCES

HOUSING

- Own home
- Apartment
- With family
- Near family
- Independent, Assisted or Continuing Care Community
- Shared Housing

FINANCIAL PLANNING

HEALTH AND LONG TERM CARE

INSURANCE

SOCIAL ACTIVITIES

LIFELONG LEARNING

PHYSICAL FITNESS

CIVIC ENGAGEMENT (VOLUNTEER)

SUPPORTIVE SERVICES

- Homemaker Services
- Home-delivered meals
- Home health Care
- Home Repair/Yard Maintenance
- Geriatric Care Management
- Transportation
- Shopping, Errands and Bill Paying
- Respite/Companion Care

Accessing information about any of these topics may be a complex and lengthy process. This is another reason why more than one person being involved in the process makes a great deal of sense.

As stated earlier, your local Area Agency on Aging is an excellent source of information as is the local Senior Center. Particularly useful in a long distance family caregiving situation, the National Elder Care

Locator at (800) 677-1116 can be very helpful. For those who are computer literate, the internet has a wealth of information on all of the above specific topics as well as many, many more. Try using key words SENIOR, CAREGIVER, or BOOMER.

Thirty years ago this vast medical and social service delivery system was not available to us when we faced the challenge of caring for my husband's parents through their terminal illnesses. However, as the old home movies reminded me, I had been empowered by my family caregiving experiences to be well grounded in the components of caring that I had come to believe mattered the most - Communication, Assistance, Respect and Empowerment. Therefore, with a well-established Communication relationship, a deep desire to respectfully share our parents life experience and Empower them to live their life with dignity and joy, we were able to provide the necessary Assistance for the remaining six years of their lives.

At first, it worked well having them live with us. Dad was quite frail, and with a new colostomy he needed significant nursing care. However, as they regained a bit of strength they soon wanted to move into their own place. We understood their desire and their belief that our own family needed a breather. So we moved them to a cute little house and they had a good few months. In some ways this was harder on us, but we all made adjustments, and we reconnected with our teenage daughters and eight year old son in a special way. They were an important part of our caregiving team.

Incidentally, there were those who questioned our involving the children in this process of intense care. We discussed this with our children and they responded with, "They're our family too!" Based on my life experience, I could only believe our current experience would have a positive impact on them. And, it did. Our three adult children have raised seven compassionate, caring young adult grandchildren. Richard and I continue to enjoy frequent interaction with all of them in person and on Facebook. We are blessed with their involvement and support as together we move through our "agewave" of challenge and change.

During this period of caring for Mom and Dad, Richard was laid off from his job, so it was necessary for me to return to work. As the doctor had predicted, mom's health declined rapidly, and other family members gladly stepped in to help. Then Dad's health failed, too, and we made the decision to choose nursing home care for his final days.

Throughout the entire time, we struggled repeatedly to piece together the many health care and support services that were needed but were in limited supply. At the end of the day, which in this case was our first major caregiving experience, we felt that we had accomplished our goal and learned a great deal in the process. That is not to say that the caregiving experience did not take its toll, it surely did! By the time Richard's parents passed away, we were all physically exhausted and emotionally, our proverbial "cup" was drained.

Over the next year as we grieved and healed I began to asses our caregiving experience. As I looked back on our struggle to care for our parents, I increasingly came to believe that difficulty with communication was at the heart of most of our struggles. We struggled with family communication as we tried to make decisions about their care, we struggled as we tried to communicate with doctors, nurses and social workers and we struggled as we tried to communicate with a fragmented service delivery system in order to access needed assistance.

Chapter 5

RESPECT
C.A.R.E. Component Three

In the context of family care issues, it is important to think about the difference between caring for minor children and caring for adult loved ones. When caring for children, the adult providing care is appropriately responsible for the decisions relative to how to best meet the care needs of the child. When participating in the care of an adult loved one, it is important to understand that unless adjudicated incompetent in a court of law, every adult has the full right to self-determination. Their loving children may not always have control over the outcome. And that is O.K. The fact that we are connected and involved in the discussion process is enough. It really is.

In fact, the fear of losing control of their own destiny is central to why the phenomenon of pulling away from family members or "circling the wagons" begins to occur. In a misguided effort to protect their independence, older adults who feel at some risk may communicate less and less with family members. The result is that at the time of a critical healthcare incident, this lack of communication makes it more difficult to help them. Loved ones may have to come from a long distance and make hasty decisions. Without complete information to meet critical care needs, the loss of control and independence unfortunately occurs just as the person had feared.

If families employ a holistic model of family care based on the previously identified essential components - **C**ommunication, **A**ssistance, **R**espect and **E**mpowerment - family relationships and the resulting quality of life for everyone will be dramatically enriched.

Understanding the real meaning and value of respect for each other's right to privacy and self-determination is a critical element in our holistic model of family care. So, let's go back to the basics. As described earlier, in the context of this model of family care, care is not something you do <u>to</u> people. The goal is not to fix everything and impose our will, but to participate with our family members in a process of collaborative, proactive life planning and decision making.

As a part of the collaborative process, respectful interpersonal behavior involves attributing real value and worth to a person's ideas, hopes, and dreams. Just as with effective communication, respect begins with a genuine sensitivity to the other person's point of view.

The process of working together respectfully also includes thinking about our own goals for wanting to care for our loved ones. Do we really want to understand what the individual perceives their needs to be and to contribute to meeting them, or do we want to get them to accept the kind of help we think they need? With an understanding of an individual's right to self-determination, it becomes clear why care decisions made without a person's active participation often run into trouble. Services put in place under these conditions might be accepted at the moment, but are often rejected later. Whenever a person feels excluded from the decision making process, anger, resentment and rejection are likely to follow.

If we accept and follow a model of care that is based on respectful collaboration and not on a need to control the outcome, we will ultimately see better results. Following a loved ones death I have never seen family members grieve over unwashed floors or dirty dishes in the sink. However, I frequently saw families grieve over broken relationships and things left unsaid.

As a part of respectful, collaborative life planning, we have the opportunity to listen and share a variety of ideas over time. Our loved one might view his/her circumstance very differently than family members and resist their input. Utilizing well established communication techniques, such as empathetic listening, we have the opportunity to soften defensive behaviors and arrive at mutually beneficial solutions. Through empathetic listening, or listening between the lines, we can expand our understanding of how the other person feels. It is important to remember feelings are neither right nor wrong; they just are! As hopes are shared and fears expressed, a better understanding of one's feelings may give clues as to how to reshape your message in a more appealing way.

In a respectful exploration of options, all participants feel free to express ideas and opinions in a nonjudgmental way. That is the essence of true brainstorming. If the person we are caring for expresses initial resistance to an idea, respect for his/her position may ultimately build trust that could lead to improved cooperation in the future. Communication channels will remain open and the fear of losing control is lessened.

Even when choices are made that we feel may not be for the best, respecting that choice and remaining involved, may make it possible to impact future decisions. Disengaging because of their refusal to see it our way simply results in a broken connection, a lost opportunity and lots of regrets in the future. A respectful and collaborative planning process leads to good outcomes.

Within a very few years following my husband's parents deaths, we had the opportunity to share many years with my mom and her husband, Fred, (Dad!) when they moved from California to Missouri to be near us. For the next fifteen years they were actively involved in the community, loved to travel and were in reasonably good health.

During this period of our lives, members of our community would frequently ask us how we managed to live in such close proximity and make our relationship work so well. I would share with them that in the beginning we made a choice to share our life experience. We established certain boundaries and agreed to respect each other's independence and differences. We recognized that it was impossible to pick up broken eggs and return them whole to the basket. It is much wiser to handle them with care and to prevent loosing what we valued.

However, the important part of the story is not what they did, but the grace with which they did it with our help. A majority of adults over 65 deal with some form of chronic impairment. We may not be able to change their circumstance; however, we hopefully can improve the person's ability to deal with it.

We began with an initial conversation about our goals and objectives. As we began to plan together for our futures, Mom and Dad indicated that they wanted to live independently for as long as possible. We agreed we would talk often and brainstorm non-judgmentally about lifestyle and healthcare choices. When choices needed to be mad, we expressed our intent to arrive at mutually agreed upon decisions, but agreed to respectfully disagree if we couldn't agree! We especially agreed to respect each other's privacy and independence. We agreed that information is power and that we would never be afraid to explore new ideas. Finally, we respectfully agreed that in the event of a major disagreement, we would not just give up, but stay in the game and work through our differences. We made this commitment in the belief that as a team, each person was well intended and had the other person's best interest at heart.

With these simple basic ground rules we shared a wonderful life together for many years. During those years, we explored, discussed the merits of and made decisions about nearly every topic one can imagine. That is not to say that all decisions were arrived at easily. However, throughout our years together, we frequently expressed appreciation to one another and reaffirmed the decision that we made to work as a team.

In our collaborative life planning relationship with my parents there were instances where we saw things differently. We early on decided to pick and choose our battles. In an effort to respect their right to self-determination, we didn't press an argument on an issue unless we believed it placed them at immediate risk. Over time this approach established an environment of trust wherein we were able to revisit issues of disagreement and ultimately achieve a mutually agreed upon choice. Central to this process is not taking rejection of your idea personally.

One issue of disagreement that we dealt with was the fact that Mom and Dad were quite adamant about their desire to remain in their own home. And, that home happened to be a large, four-bedroom, multistoried house with several sets of stairs both inside and out, a three-car garage, built on a hillside!

But at the time' staying in their own home was very important to them.

Eventually Dad developed severe arthritis, and mom had a problem with her heart. We began to observe their changing capabilities and had some concerns as to how realistic remaining in their own home would be over the long term. However, in view of their strong feelings on the matter, we decided to respect their wishes and back away from this issue for a while.

Though we often wished we could just place them in a protective bubble, we knew that wasn't possible. Even more than with growing children, we could protect them only to a point. Regarding certain issues we simply had to step back, respect their view of the world and be ready for next opportunity to explore other options

Of course this does involve elements of risk. This is where it is important that becoming comfortable with possible outcomes that may not meet our ideal hopes comes into play. We came to a place where we made the choice that if we remained on good terms and stayed connected, for us, it was good enough.

Following bypass surgery, knee and hip replacement surgery and a couple of falls going down the hillside to get the paper, they were ready to talk about the "house" subject again. In a discussion after dinner one evening, we began to explore what constitutes "home" at any given time. We encouraged them to think of choosing a home that would meet their current needs and would create opportunities for continued independence rather than have to deal with unnecessary barriers in the future.

We talked about the early years of my mother's marriage to my father. They lived in a cute little apartment close to work because they didn't have a car. This apartment met their needs and was "home" for a few years. But when I was born, they needed more room, so they bought a nice two bedroom house.

For a few years that met their needs and it was our "home." Then my brother Jack came along and we moved to a three bedroom house with a big yard and a pool. This met our needs perfectly and was "home" for many years. The key element in the choices made was always their need at that particular time of life.

After our conversation about why people choose different houses at various points in their lives, it became clear to all of us that a big house built on a hillside with many steps to the basement no longer met their changing needs. They were ready to start looking for a new house – a house that would meet their needs for the future and would become their new "home.

During the last ten years of their lives, between mother and dad, they dealt with cataract surgery, two knee replacements, one hip replacement, two heart bypass surgeries, Leukemia and Alzheimer's disease. With our assistance they made good lifestyle choices that enabled them to enjoy their independence for several more years.

Richard and I helped them downsize, or as I prefer to say "smartsize," from a two story, four bedroom home to a two bedroom duplex next to us. A few years later, we all moved from Missouri to smaller homes in Arizona. Ultimately they chose a new "home" in an assisted care setting for the last months of their lives.

Following our holistic model of family care, utilizing effective communication and appropriate assistance in a respectful way Mom and dad were empowered to reach mutually beneficial choices. When we have the opportunity to participate in shaping our future at any age we are always happier with the outcome.

As a result of our decision to commit to a respectful shared life experience, we all enjoyed a full range of extended opportunities. We traveled, fished, gardened, enjoyed lifelong learning and volunteer opportunities and continued to care for Granny Clara until she died at ninety six. All the while we had the opportunity to share the blessing of our growing family of grandchildren and great grandchildren.

My parents wise choice to stay connected to supportive family, assured their ability to live a rich independent life for many, many years. Mom and Dad were fortunate enough to live well into their eighties. When chronic illness and disability finally limited their ability to function independently our caring relationship was well developed and we were able to make decisions together about how to again meet their changing needs.

Midway in our journey of caring for my parents, something occurred in our family that we are beginning to see in families with increased frequency. The caregiving role next enveloped our children who are members of what is coming to be known as the Sandwich Generation.

The changing face of aging, where science and modern medicine are making it possible for us to live into our eighties and nineties, has created a new phenomenon where middle aged adults are likely to be participating in the care of their own growing children, their parents and even their grandparents. Our adult children fit into this category. "The Sandwich Generation" if born born between 1946 and 1964 are also referred to as "Boomers" Having been born during the big baby boom following World II.

There are approximately 76 million "Boomers" who might be caught in this circumstance of "Sandwich" caregiving. Clearly, being in the role of caregiver for more than one generational member of the family at the same time can create great stress. However, by utilizing this innovative, holistic model of family care, wherein all participants respect each other's independence and boundaries, families can effectively meet each other's need for assistance and move toward a richer quality of life for everyone.

As an integral part of our family's proactive approach to family care, our adult children had been a part of the ongoing shared life experience with their grandparents. As teenagers and as young adults beginning to raise their own families they had remained involved in helping us to care for both their maternal and paternal grandparents, though primarily in a supportive role. This natural growth toward a collaborative partnership in caregiving is obviously the ideal way to move into proactive care planning.

However, these techniques can easily be learned and implemented at any point in life's journey. As Mya Angelou the noted author, poet, and philosopher says, "When we know better, we do better." Our family's next generation was about to assume a more active role in our family's care.

While still in Missouri, prior to Richard's and my retirement, I had begun to experience some health problems. In keeping with our proactive way of looking at possible future care needs, we began to think ahead. Here we were currently dealing with issues related to my parents increasing care needs and now in my late fifties, I was beginning to experience health problems of my own.

Caregivers usually focus fully on their caregiving responsibilities and often neglect their own health and well-being. We read more and more about "caregiver burnout" and how the caregiver can succumb to health problems before the loved one for whom they are caring.

This comes under the heading of respecting your own needs. If you don't take care of yourself, you won't be able to take care of anyone else. I recalled what I had always thought were my mom's natural instincts to prioritize everyone's needs and not become martyr to any one of them. Or, perhaps she also she grew into this wisdom overtime as I did.

We routinely see growing numbers of chronic illness in caregivers which are often stress induced. Such was clearly the case in our family and it was beginning to take a toll on me. This signaled an alert. We began to think once again about developing a care plan that would include multiple layers of support that would endure over time and make it easier for our children to help us.

Though my health had stabilized for the time being, my instincts to think ahead kicked into gear. As it turned out, my inclination to plan ahead with regard to care issues served us well once again.

As much as we might like to have things remain the same, they rarely do for very long. Again, we experienced health care issues that challenged our multitiered family care team. We needed all their support and encouragement to negotiate both a complex service delivery system and the emotional hurdles we faced.

Our oldest daughter Julie had already made one trip from Arizona to Missouri to help us when I had a hip replacement and another when her grandmother had heart by-pass surgery. I began to think about how difficult it was for Julie to have to travel such distance to participate actively in our care.

It would be so much easier if we were all living in the same community. Unquestionably, we could still live our own independent lives. However, the best way to plan realistically to assure that we were well prepared for the changes and challenges that might occur was to consider relocating closer to our children. It all just seemed so logical to me. By relocating closer to Julie, we could increase the joys of sharing our lives and lessen the difficulties encountered in long distance caregiving.

Having been transferred to Missouri thirty years earlier by my husband's company, we had always hoped to retire to a warmer climate. In family discussions through the years about our plans for retirement, Julie and her husband Papu had often suggested relocating to Arizona to be closer to them.

It was becoming clear that all of our children and their

spouses were actively living our holistic view of care through a shared life experience with their own immediate and extended families. Papu's mother, a retired physician from India, had already come to live near them and now they were inviting us to join them. Our second daughter Kim's family lived near her husband's family and was able to help them as needed. Our son Rick and his wife Eva enjoyed a shared life experience with her widowed mother.

Relocating closer to your adult children in your later retirement years rather than moving farther away can be a smart move. It shows respect for your children's lives with regard to their primary responsibilities for employment and raising their family, while it eases the burden on them of long distance caregiving. It also means that you have the pleasure of enjoying your family on a regular basis.

The early years of retirement can be filled with many opportunities for fun, travel, second careers and lifelong learning. However, sociologists say that more frail elderly are at greater risk from isolation than any disease. Studies show that those older adults who stay connected with family and community and remain comfortable with change age the most successfully.

A cautionary note at this point might be appropriate. A holistic model of family care by its very nature is not accomplished quickly. However, the results in the long term are infinitely more rewarding. Remember, we are talking about developing a solid infrastructure of mutually interdependent family members who actively participate in collaborative, proactive life planning with older family members to assure a high quality of life with dignity, respect and as much independence as possible.

So, as they say, it was back to the drawing board. We sat down with my parents and presented a range of options for them to consider. After several months, we all decided to join Julie and Papu in Arizona.

With this move we would have the opportunity to

continue to live independent, rewarding lives and enjoy the added benefit of additional family support. Every parent says that they don't want to be a burden to their children. The surest way to accomplish this goal is to take proactive measures to minimize the imposition should we require their help.

Recalling the *"Agewave"* phenomenon occurring in our modern aging culture, where increasingly there is more than one generation in a family dealing with the opportunities and challenges of aging, our families experience was not unique. In view of this *"Agewave"* phenomenon, where we are likely to face healthcare incidents and recover to good health many times as we age, the strategy of incorporating a multidisciplinary, multigenerational model of family care into our lives simply makes good sense. Assistance from caring family members in helping to find, evaluate and obtain healthcare and support services result in the best and most complete assistance.

Over the next year, we sold our homes and moved to Arizona, into new homes in the same neighborhood as Julie and Papu. This process in itself involved elements of stress, drama and humor. Such a time was when we were at odds as to how to organize things as we prepared for our move to Arizona. With the need to pack everything from two houses in preparation for the movers, planning for the process was critical. Naturally, since mom was eighty two at the time, I assumed that Richard and I would do all the packing. Oh no, she insisted she and dad would do their own packing.

This could have been a major confrontation. As I pondered how to deal with this situation, I began to think about how I would feel if I were in her shoes. Then I began to think outside of the box as we found ourselves doing more and more. How can we make this a win, win situation? Respecting their views, we met in the middle which often happened. The result was that they did some of their own packing. I planned the packing timeline with an extra three days lead.

On the designated day for packing to be completed, if in fact it was, we would all have a nice break until moving day. As it turned out, their packing wasn't complete. They were very frustrated and quite ready for some help. We all had a good laugh. Together, we got back to work and were packed and ready to go on moving day. Central to a happy outcome, when we chose to use a team approach, was a willingness to put ourselves in the other person's place and negotiate a solution that respects everyone's needs.

Should families struggle with efforts to work together collaboratively, there are professionals who specialize in these areas. Geriatric care managers are listed both on the internet and in the yellow pages. Care coordinators can be located through Area Agencies on Aging and Senior Centers. Finally, Family Mediation is a growing area of counseling that can be quite effective.

Certainly, if our loved one has lost the ability to manage their own affairs and may be a risk to themselves or others, then we as family members have a responsibility to take appropriate action on their behalf. Attorneys who specialize in Eldercare Law or public agencies that specialize in elder abuse and neglect prevention are good sources of help in sorting out these issues. These services can be accessed through regional Area Agencies on Aging.

Our efforts to interact respectfully with loved ones for whom we care creates a rich environment in which we can carry out the most rewarding part of what any caring experience. In my opinion, to empower the person for whom we care to enjoy their life to the fullest is what it is all about. From early childhood parents strive to empower their children to achieve their full potential. It is exactly the same when caring for another person. I was reminded of this as I replaced the reels of old movie film I had been reviewing back in the box.

At the bottom of the box, probably placed there by my mom, almost as cushioning for these old films, were two of my favorite old soft children's books. I thumbed through the pages and my heart was flooded with so many wonderful, warm memories of my childhood. As I scanned their titles, two central themes jumped out at me. I recognized them as ones that had influenced much of my life.

Chapter 6

EMPOWERMENT

C.A. R. E. Component Four

I looked at the cover of the book, "*The Little Engine That Could.*" I almost heard the little blue engine singing "I think I can, I think I can". Moving on to "*The Wizard of Oz,*" tears nearly came to my eyes as I imagined Glenda the Good Witch saying to Dorothy, "You have the power, you've always had the power!" With these words Mom had always encouraged me to pursue the dreams of my heart.

Empowering anyone to achieve the dreams of their heart is a richly satisfying accomplishment. I find it interesting that as we raise our children the entire process is focused on helping them develop and use the skills necessary to live meaningful and happy lives. But as we begin caring for our parents or other adult loved ones, it seems the primary focus is helping to get supportive services to assure their safety and well-being. I suppose this is understandable when we consider that most people enter into the caregiving role at a time of critical need for supportive services.

However, in keeping with our holistic concept of caring, empowering our elderly loved ones toward achieving a happy, meaningful quality of life can be the most fulfilling and rewarding component of care.

Of course, this is easier when patterns of strong interpersonal relationships have been maintained throughout adulthood. Then empowering behaviors are well established and routinely used. However, the caring process can be improved at any point if there is a mental shift toward enriching the quality of life rather than just physical caregiving. Just like any life changing improvement it is never too late and it then can establish a pattern of family interaction that will continue on with each generation.

I feel confident in saying that my parents decision to enter into shared life planning early in their retirement contributed greatly to the quality of their later years and the ease with which we made our move to Arizona. During the first couple of years in Arizona, we enjoyed getting settled and involved in our new community.

Having retired once, Richard became reemployed and enjoyed a five year second career. I become involved in a lifelong learning organization and some professional consulting activities at our local community college.

Mom and dad got involved with their new church. She volunteered as an Ombudsman at a local

nursing home. Having always been the one in the family to whom everyone came for emotional support, it was quite natural to see her advocate on behalf of nursing home residents. She did this for several years and at one point was honored as volunteer of the year. Central to the concept of empowerment in our mature years, is recognizing and then utilizing these natural gifts as our circumstances change.

Then, having been diagnosed with Diabetes a few years earlier, I suddenly suffered a major heart attack followed by quintuple bypass surgery.

Needless to say, our proactive approach to our family care needs found us in a good place to deal with such a traumatic healthcare occurrence. The depth of support in our multigenerational family meant that Julie and her family provided comfort and emotional support to my parents as well as critical direct care for me during a lengthy and difficult recovery.

The fact that we were not only living in the same

community, but in four houses in a row empowered Julie to move with relative ease between houses as she helped with my physical care, comforted and reassured my parents and helped her son Justin get ready for his big prom night. Justin had learned to dance with Grams at her eightieth birthday party several years ago. What an example of "Sandwich Generation" caregiving!

The value of the role played by all members of one's family absolutely cannot be overstated. In most families, the family member living nearest to the parents usually takes the lead in caregiving activities. This makes good sense as they can respond most quickly and stay in close touch on a regular basis. In families where there is solid cooperation, this plan works well when other family members agree to support the action of the primary caregiver who lives in close proximity to the person needed care... Naturally, there is the understanding that all family members have been a part of establishing the basic care plan to be followed and are a part of making any major changes to the plan.

In our family each of the children played very supportive roles to us and to each other at various stages of our caregiving journey and each brought very unique gifts to the process.

According to Webster, empowerment involves increasing ones spiritual, social or political strength, often through increasing ones confidence. This relates directly to our self-esteem or belief in our ability to do something well.

As we age, and especially as we approach retirement, the concept of feeling empowered to embrace a new lifestyle seems to be a natural. We are leaving a period in our lives, usually marked by high productivity and value and will be transitioning to a new lifestyle that will be marked by ample time to pursue many of the things we have been waiting all our lives to do. It really doesn't require a great deal of encouragement.

Typically, it is when we are challenged by changes in our health or losses of functional capabilities that we must face limitations that affect our ability to enjoy the activities we had come to love. Problems with our eyesight might limit our ability to drive. Arthritis could impact our ability to enjoy golf. Central to aging is the loss continuum of physical abilities, jobs, family roles, control, and independence. These losses can lead to a corresponding loss of value, severe depression and decline into isolation. Empowering behaviors in a caring relationship can stimulate an individual to explore alternative options that can lead to entirely new and rewarding experiences.

A good friend, who could no longer golf because of severe arthritis, was encouraged to share her experience with teenagers participating in a community golf clinic. She was not only able to continue to enjoy a sport she loved but having been a teacher, she was able to inspire and empower young athletes to accomplish their goals. Her success as a mentor to young golfers, in turn inspired her to seek other opportunities to mentor young people. This circular component to the concept of empowerment gives it real added value. It is an enhanced sense of self-esteem that leads us to feel more in control of our life and less a victim when we are faced with the challenges of aging.

This ability to empower someone can become of an ever increasing importance as a central element in our changing life experience. As chronic illness or disability becomes a part of our changing reality, disengagement and isolation can place our loved one at risk of premature decline. Empowering them to recognize, redirect and use changing abilities in a meaningful way can validate life experience and result in rich opportunities.

With my heart attack and quintuple bypass surgery,

Julie played a central role during the critical incident itself and physical recovery. The unfailing gift of love and encouragement empowered me to see opportunities for growth and renewal in what could have been a devastating and defeating health crisis at the early age of fifty nine.

At one particularly low point in a long, challenging recovery, it took a particularly stern approach by my daughter Kim to set me back on the track of "little engine that could". Since Julie had been my primary caregiver, she had become particularly sensitive to the significant pain and suffering I had been experiencing during a very long and difficult recovery. Her gentle comfort and sensitivity had brought me so far.

During a visit from Kim, she and Julie discussed the fears and anxieties I was experiencing. At just the right moment, and coming from a different perspective, her empowering intervention encouraged me to pull my self up by the boot straps as the saying goes and get back in the game. Thanks for the individual gifts we each have to give to one another.

Out of my own difficult health crisis, I was led to redirect my energies toward an ever expanding view of our changing life experience. As my health began to improve I began to explore meaningful ways that I could improve my chances for future good health and well-being.

I began participating in a broad array of preventative health strategies recommended as a part of my cardiac rehabilitation. I was empowered by my family to pay more attention to my own needs, one of my own routine admonitions to caregivers, i.e., to take better care of themselves. I was encouraged to nurture my own spirit and feed my dreams.

This led me to explore renewed interest in lifelong learning programs offered through our community college. Also, with their encouragement, I was empowered to begin writing about my passion for encouraging families to provide a more holistic approach to caring for their loved ones through strengthened family relationships. I began to share this empowering message at caregiver conferences and as always happens with empowering behaviors, was enriched by the stories of success that came back to me.

During this period of time, we became increasingly aware that my precious mother was exhibiting alarming changes in her behavior. These changes in behavior resulted in the sad diagnosis of Alzheimer's.

 Again, gathered together as a team and considered our options for the future. Even in the case of dealing with the dreaded Alzheimer's disease, we dealt respectfully and openly with our new information, treating it as a source of power and not a threat. Mom felt empowered to be a true part of the planning process because we began by listening to her response to the diagnosis, listening to how she felt and her hopes for the future.

Naturally, mom hoped she would be able to stay at home with dad as long as possible. Because we lived right next door, this sounded quite reasonable. As we should have expected, Mom also hoped that she and dad would be able to stay together when the time came that her care needs could no longer be met at home.

The rest of our conversation dealt with the several things they hoped to do while they could. Due to the long term trust that had been established between us and the open way we considered future options, they moved forward into these uncharted waters with calm and dignity.

Confronting such a dreaded prospect as Alzheimer's, in an environment of trust and openness, minimizes the fear aspect and maximizes the opportunity to prepare for and deal with change in a proactive way. As a family we began to seek the best information on treatment and care options. Information is power and empowering. We participated in and were strengthened by friendships shared in support groups. Rather than spending the next few years in denial, we eased into the experience and cherished the many good times while preparing for Mom's changing needs.

For Mother, we believed the progress of the disease was slowed by medications, and various behavior modification techniques. As a family, we encouraged her to view her past life experience as a valuable legacy to be shared with her children and grandchildren. She got involved in a scrap booking group and she enjoyed sorting through and organizing old photos in keepsake albums, adding comments about the events that only she could remember. Using the activity as a life review process, it turned out to be a pleasurable, therapeutic and validating pastime for her. Additionally, it left an invaluable and treasured gift for our family.

Even toward the end, when they had moved into a lovely little apartment in a special Alzheimer's community, residents were empowered to participate in appropriate activities such as gardening in waist level flower beds, social and fitness activities and animal care. The community was designed so that residents had free access to outdoor patios as all paths began and ended in their hall or community as it was called community. Their community had a nautical theme and was called Boatyard Cove.

It is worthy of note, in keeping with our proactive approach, Julie and I began our search for just the right Alzheimer's care facility several months before we had a need for it. We enjoyed meals there ahead of time, regularly used the beauty shop and routinely took part in the social activities. When, because of mother's wandering and other safety issues, more supervision was needed, mom and dad were welcomed to their new neighborhood by their friends and it was a gentle transition.

 Mom's, natural caregiving instincts surfaced in the dining room and until the last weeks of her life she looked after her friends, making sure the servers were aware of who needed more coffee or tea.

As her condition progressed, we spent more and more time reflecting on the wonderful times we had all shared together, reminiscing about specific events, vacations and parties. In fact, in retrospect, I must say, it was when mom was either planning or hosting a great family party that she was at her happiest.

It was no surprise that she was very specific about how she wanted to be remembered following her death. She hoped we would have a brief memorial service followed by a "beach party," a family reunion at the beach. In her party planning mode she even suggested we wait about six months. And, so it would be. Now, she was empowering me to go toward the future as she was prepared to do. She reminded me that just as we had been through so much together, she would be beside me at the beach.

We were truly blessed that mother's nature remained unchanged throughout the progression of the disease.

She remained positive, highly social and knew us all. During the last three weeks, she lost most of her functional capabilities including the ability to swallow. On Julie's frequent visits, she often brought fresh fruit which mom dearly loved. The last morsels of food she enjoyed were four plump, juicy grapes a week before she died. She delicately placed them in her mouth with her beautifully manicured fingers, chewed them with great relish and easily swallowed them with a smile on her face.

During one of our last conversations mother made one valiant last effort to shape her future, and truth be told, she may have had that impact. As we walked in the garden, mom shared how she had tried to never pray selfishly. She wondered if she was praying selfishly if she prayed that God would not "make her stick around for the end of this Alzheimer's thing." I assured her that her prayer was not a selfish one. I told her I would even join her in her prayer.

We approached Easter week, Hospice was called in

and Mother's worn out little body lay motionless in her bed. The morning of Easter Eve, her caregiver came by and prepared to bathe her. I remembered I had just bought her a lovely new yellow, floral cotton gown for spring. I took it from the dresser drawer and laid it carefully across the foot of the bed. As her caregiver Sandy gently bathed her, she quietly sang the old hymn, "His Eye Is on the Sparrow." I glanced over and noticed dad quietly sipping lemonade Sandy had brought in along with a small plate of sugar cookies for him before beginning mom's bath. Everything was amazingly right with our little world.

Then, Julie and I rubbed her favorite Ester Lauder scented lotion all over her fragile, relaxed little body before placing the new yellow gown over her head. We settled and smoothed it before placing her hands gently over the edge of the fresh, folded sheet. I opened the window just a bit in preparation for the moment that mom's sweet spirit would be ready to fly away. A gentle, warm and welcoming breeze floated into the room. Our lovely pre-Easter "spa" experience refreshed and prepared us all for this next passage on life's journey.

As Julie kissed her grandmother lightly before leaving to get some dinner, Mom whispered, "I love you! You know I've always loved you." Within hours, before the dawn of Easter morn, my precious mother's prayer was answered and she was freed from "having to stick around for the end of this Alzheimer's thing."

Chapter 7

GATHER AT THE BEACH

Grief is a natural and healing process. It can, however, be fraught with much pain and may be prolonged and sometimes endless when there have been emotional separations and unresolved issues prior to a death. When families choose to share even the difficult issues experienced during truly caring relationships, the grief experienced when death occurs is most always limited and fades appropriately with time.

Needless to say, the weeks and months following Mom's death were difficult and I missed her terribly. However, our sorrow over losing her soon shifted toward encouraging dad to move toward life again. Since he had been so focused on being her "dear and loving companion" during her long struggle with Alzheimer's, we were concerned about how he would make the adjustment to living without her.

As most families who have lived through Alzheimer's know, it is referred to as "the long good-bye." Having made peace with his good-byes some time ago, Dad seemed to be quite ready to move forward with life. It is important to note, that when you move toward the future with no regrets and many happy memories, the journey forward is easier. Dad's desire to re-engage in life as a tribute to Mother, helped him to make the transition in a healthy positive way.

We helped Dad select a lovely assisted living community. Then, decorated his apartment with lots of pictures, and keepsakes of their great life together. We watched him settle in and quickly make new friends and become involved in a variety of social and therapeutic activities. We were all thrilled with his determination to live well in honor of Mom's memory. However, he often talked of how much he missed her and longed to see her again. Therefore, when within the year his fragile little body wore out, we knew he was grateful to be able to rejoin her in a better place.

As we moved through the months following his death, and life returned to a gentler pace, our appetite for life returned. We began to think about the beach party hoped we have. The planning began and soon arrangements were made for family and friends to gather at the beach to honor her life well lived.

Our cousins Janet and Steve owned a beautiful house along the California coast. They suggested this might be a great place for our beach party. Mom and Dad often vacationed there and it would be conveniently located for many of those we knew would want to come.

Once the date and place were established, invitations were sent. We let everyone know that we understood that the timing may not work for everyone. As with all Mom's parties, we would understand if some couldn't make it and we would celebrate double for those who could not join us. We knew that they would be there with us in spirit.

Most of the younger families with children stayed at the house, while hotel reservations were made at a lovely inn a few blocks away for others. Everything was soon in readiness for the party to begin.

Most of Mom's immediate family and friends arrived to share in the small memorial service that had been thoughtfully arranged by her youngest sister Ethel before gathering at the beach. One of her nephews, in his eulogy, referenced the meter maid who ticketed those who had not put enough coins in the parking meter. He reminded us that there was never a meter running on Mom's time. She was always available for those who needed her, without any limit.

Representatives from all of Mom's six sister's

families were there and we all enjoyed a meal together after the service. While everyone was savoring dessert and sipping coffee, the reminiscing began. Each story was better than the one before, embellished I'm sure with color and humor as often happens to stories told many times over. The room rang with laughter and swayed with tear drenched hugs.

The party had begun and Mother was surely present in that place. From there it was on to the beach where we would be joined by many others who wished to celebrate her life with us. Some came for the full four days. Some came for just a few hours. They all gifted us with their presence and added to the joy we experienced.

After a restful sleep, it was a joyous and comforting feeling to waken to a wonderful sea breeze, children's laughter and the aroma of coffee wafting in from the kitchen. A quick splash of water on my face, an exchanged wink with my mom's reflection in the mirror and I joined those in the kitchen for a lovely start to the day. And, so, the party began!

Some of those gathered were already planning a walk out on the pier to do a little souvenir shopping, while a few of those who hadn't seen each other for some time were quietly chatting and catching up on what was going on in each of their lives. Some of the nieces had realized that my cousin Bette would be celebrating her sixtieth birthday while we were all at the beach together. Oh boy, another chance for a party within a party. So they were off to the store for the fixings of a mini Mexican fiesta.

The days passed as relationships were rekindled, new friendships made and at the center of it all, Mother's caring spirit moved freely. As I moved from group to group and shared in all the fun, I remembered yet another conversation with mom during her last days.

We were sitting together on the patio and sharing our thoughts about what was to come when our time on Earth came to an end. Mom felt very certain that she would see us down here going on about our business. I wasn't quite so sure. I expressed some skepticism about the many reports I had heard of people who claim that you can communicate with those who crossed over, as they say. I confessed that I had never had such an experience. I suggested that it would really be great if she would communicate with me from the other side. She responded by assuring me that she would. However, she cautioned me to remember to be listening. During this special time together at the beach, I felt her presence, but had not yet heard her voice.

While the cousins and grandchildren splashed in the surf, most of them shared stories about how mom had taught them all to swim in her big pool. She was only able to do this after she herself overcame her fear of water and learned to swim at the age of fifty. She chose to do this when she and my father bought a house with a pool. Mom felt a responsibility to ensure that all thirty four nieces and nephews could safely enjoy fun in the pool.

In our great family tradition of oral storytelling, everyone had a story to share. The youngsters of the group learned some new life lessons by hearing them first hand with all the passion and depth of meaning that oral storytelling conveys. It seemed funny to think about the fact that with Mother gone, we were now the "tribal elders" charged with leading the way for the next generation. Again, we laughed much and cried some as we recalled the past while sharing dreams of the future.

We celebrated my cousin Bette's sixtieth birthday with a wonderful Mexican dinner. Then we piled on sofas, chairs, stools, pillows, and every available surface. We sprawled on the floor in the living room, dining room and adjacent family room. We watched a beautiful video my cousin Jim had lovingly put together. It chronicled Mom's extraordinary life.

The images we enjoyed viewing, reminded me that mom's life certainly encompassed all of the four key components of "effective caregiving." Her open, straightforward way of communicating invited easy exchange of ideas and feelings. She always listened with genuine interest. The video showed so many examples of how she was ready to assist friends and family in both big and little ways.

Mother held all members of her family in high esteem and truly valued their sometimes diverse lifestyles and varied points of view. Her deep respect for the individuality of others made it possible for her to "sift the chaff from the wheat and let the chaff blow away." Her greatest joy always seemed to be in mentoring someone to help him achieve his highest potential. Whether it was teaching children to swim or advocating on behalf of the rights of nursing home residents, Mom's efforts to empower those around her never ended.

As the video drew to a close, there was much discussion of what we had all learned from her as she touched our lives in her special ways. We all made quiet little vows to continue to live in the spirit of her exemplary life. Everyone acknowledged that Mother's life had not been an easy life. Indeed it had its fair share of all the trials and tribulations most people face. The central message to be found in the way she cared for those she loved was that maintaining relationships with those she cared about meant more than any single issue of the moment. There were no broken relationships in Mother's life, just relationships that grew and evolved over time.

Sunrise on the last morning of our time together at the beach dawned with a special brilliance. It was almost as if God was setting the stage for a grand finale. The aroma of fresh coffee drew me once again where several were gathered on the patio enjoying pastries and mixed tropical fruit with zabaglione. The succulent taste of fragrant ripe mango, pineapple and juicy red strawberries settled on my palette with a pleasure that was to foretell the rest of my day.

There was an excitement in the air and the mood of

those gathered in the morning sun was one of appreciation and joy at having shared this time together. Friends and relatives talked of returning home to their busy lives, but especially of when they would see each other again and how they would certainly stay in touch. Then it was down to the shore one last time.

As we strolled toward the incoming tide, our toes squished in the sand in that funny, familiar way. The youngsters were busy building sand castles and trying to bury each other in the sand. A few of the guys were trying to get a sand volleyball game going. We gals were content to stroll along the beach and treasure these last moments together.

The breeze was brisk and the salty air felt good on our skin as we once again reflected on the great value of sharing these experiences in our lives. We all pretty much agreed that passing along the meaning of a caring shared life experience was one of the primary responsibilities of "tribal elders."

Each generation, as they have been inspired by the generation before, will interpret and then shape their own caring experience and live so that their examples inspire the next generation.

The holistic concept of caring based on **C**ommunication, **A**ssistance, **R**espect and **E**mpowerment is one that requires a full family investment. It really starts with family conversations about how we wish to care for each other and how we want to be cared for. There are no rights or wrongs. However, those who actively strive toward this goal will ultimately know the joy and contentment that can be the result of such efforts.

We strolled across the wet sand together. I began to focus on the shells that were being washed up on the sand and decided to collect a few as keepsakes of this precious moment in time. As I began to pick up shells, I noticed that there seemed to be an unusual number of perfect, unbroken shells on this stretch of beach. As

I filled my pockets and admired the variety of shapes and colors I glimpsed a partially buried Sand dollar. I gently scooped it up and examined the beautiful markings on its surface. Sand dollars didn't appear very often. I had walked this beach so many times and never saw this abundance and variety of finely marked shells before.

I called to my cousin Bette to join me in admiring my wonderful discovery. They were so beautiful and perfect. As Bette approached to share in my pleasure, I glanced to the right and picked up a perfect Starfish. Its texture was unusually varied and it was brilliant in color. Oh my God, my eyes spied yet another Starfish. Then I spotted a gorgeous, perfectly shaped Slipper Limpet, my mother's favorite seashell.

All of a sudden, I remembered her admonition to "Listen." Tears began to stream down my face as

Bette and I hugged. It felt like I was being showered with earthly evidence of Mother's love. She was speaking to me in a perfectly clear voice. I was enveloped by her presence and wrapped in her love.

When I finally glanced up, my daughters Julie and Kim were rushing over to see what all the commotion was about. They too were amazed with our fantastic find and everyone proceeded to gather keepsakes of our wonderful time together. With my pockets bulging with precious treasure from the sea and my daughters by my side, we walked across the beach and returned to the house.

Cars were being loaded with luggage and sunburned but happy people for return trips to airports and waiting homes. Amid hugs and much chatter, we bid our friends and family a tearful farewell

and in the words of the old books of my childhood, "All's well that ends well."

A few weeks later I spoke to my daughters, Julie and Kim, about the depth of emotion I experienced that last glorious morning on the sun drenched shore. I shared with them what I believed had been this amazing expression of caring I had received from my mother. Mom's message of caring and love remains with me each day. I continue to listen for her comfort and guidance. Hopefully, this story of my family's shared life journey will inspire and empower you as you care for one another.

AFTERWORD

Ten years have passed since our family gathered at the beach to celebrate my mom's life.

During these years, we have enjoyed parties for Richard's eightieth birthday, our Golden Wedding Anniversary and Julie and Papu's Silver Anniversary. We attended our grandchildren's high school graduations and observed the earning of two Baccalaureates and one Master's Degree.

Intermittent health challenges have created ripples in our ongoing *"Agewave."* However, with our unswerving holistic approach to caring for one another, we continue to enjoy a rich and fulfilling shared life journey with our precious family

ABOUT THE AUTHOR

While happily raising two teenage daughters and an eight year old son, JoAnn Freeborn was thrust into the challenge of caring for her husband's parents who were both terminally ill with cancer. Five years later, upon their deaths, she determined to devote her future energy to making every effort to help others who were caring for their loved ones.

She returned to school and earned a B.S. in Mass Communications. She did her graduate study at Oxford University in England, and ultimately served as Executive Director of Region Ten Area Agency on Aging.

During her tenure, JoAnn never saw families grieve over dirty floors or unwashed dishes following the death of a loved one. She did however, comfort many families grieving over broken relationships and unspoken words. Therefore, she developed and implemented a unique, holistic approach to effective and mutually beneficial caregiving based on strengthening family relations as an essential component.